PLAN THE LIFE YOU WANT

A 7-Step Plan To Achieve Your Goals

TK OWENS

PLAN THE LIFE YOU WANT

A 7-Step Plan To Achieve Your Goals

TK OWENS

Plan the Life You Want

A 7-Step Plan To Achieve Your Goals

TK Owens

Copyright © 2020 by TK Owens

All rights reserved. No part of this book may be reproduced or transmitted in any form or by any means, electronic or mechanical, including photocopying, or by any information storage or retrieval system, without written permission from the publisher.

ISBN: 978-1-7361671-0-6

Website: tkoconsultingllc.com

Dedication

I would like to dedicate this book to my late and beloved father, Julius Pratt Jr. It was on October 21, 2020, that I finished writing my book, on the first anniversary of my father's passing on October 21, 2019.

It is amazing what can be accomplished in one year.

Look Daddy, I am an Author! I hope you are proud.

Acknowledgements

First and foremost, I have to give credit and all praises to God. I am grateful for it all; for the highs and lows, for all of the unexpected blessings and setbacks. Without the obstacles that were placed in my life, I would not have the opportunity to grow and learn. So for that, I am grateful for the woman you have groomed me to be.

Secondly, I would like to thank my writing coach, Dennard Mitchell for cheering me on through this journey and for your weekly check-ins and holding me accountable to cross the finish line.

A huge thanks go to my girls (you know who you are) who witnessed me placing this goal on my vision board and for always supporting and believing in me.

I would like to also thank my Mom, Linda and Grandmother, Barbara who instilled in me the true meaning of hard work and dedication. I watched you for years, working non-stop to provide for me and even though you spoiled me and gave me everything I ever wanted, I hope in return, that I made you proud. Now it is time for me to take care of you.

And, filled with emotion, I must thank my children Darrin, Darria, Farrel III and Fakih for just being you and accepting me for who I am and being the best mom I could be to you. You motivate me every day to want more and be a good example for you to follow.

Last but not least, I would like to thank my husband and best friend, Farrel Owens for being my support system. Thank you for loving me and being you even when I thought you were hard on me; you see things in me that I sometimes do not see in myself. You continue to push me to great heights and encourage me when I need it the most. I look up to you more than you know and admire your tenacity and ambition to succeed. And, I know with our love for one another, we can accomplish anything.

Table of Contents

INTRODUCTION 1
GETTING STARTED 7
ABOUT THE BOOK 14
STEP 1: KNOW WHAT YOU WANT 21
STEP 2: SET YOUR GOALS 32
STEP 3: CREATE A PLAN 44
STEP 4: TAKE ACTION 52
STEP 5: BE READY! 61
STEP 6: DON'T GIVE UP 68
STEP 7: BE YOU! 77
WRAPPING UP 86
ABOUT THE AUTHOR 92
TESTIMONIALS 94

PLAN THE LIFE YOU WANT

A 7-Step Plan To Achieve Your Goals

TK OWENS

INTRODUCTION

I've decided to write this book to help those that may be struggling with knowing what they want out of life. As a child, we are often asked, "what do you want to be when you grow up?" As a child, do we really know? The only thing that life has taught us at five years old is to play, eat, and sleep. I believe that "life" itself is the best teacher, and molds us to become the person that God uniquely designs us to be.

Jeremiah 1:5 says, *"I knew you before I formed you in your mother's womb. Before you were born, I set you apart and appointed you as my prophet to the nations."*

I truly believe the experiences we endure (good, bad, tragic or life-changing) are all strategically planned by God with the hope to shape our characters. We have the power to change any behavior we do not deem fit, not only to others but to ourselves.

Even in worse situations, we have the ability to see the good if you love the Lord as stated in **Romans 8:28** *"And we know that in all things God works for the good of those who love him, who have been called according to his purpose."*

The year 2020 has been nothing but a year of challenges, as our entire country is going through unprecedented times filled with uncertainty as the Coronavirus has killed thousands. We have been subjected to isolation and no human contact with a stay at home order. Just as we thought things could not get any worst, we find ourselves in the middle of a race war for injustice amongst Black Americans because of police brutalities and senseless killings.

And, as bad as things are right now, the name, George Floyd, who was tragically murdered by police from the Minneapolis Police Department has changed the world. Even amid the chaos, good has come out of his tragic death. Millions of people from every work of life all over the world have come together in unity to fight for equality, and justice during the Black Lives Matter Movement. Laws are being reformed and changed for the better, and we are getting back to a

New Normal in the best way we know.

To give you a personal testimony, as I write this book, everything that could go wrong is going wrong! Let us see. Where do I begin? I lost my father due to his third massive stroke in October, buried him on my birthday in November. I faced some challenges in my marriage in March, the Coronavirus hit, and we had to stay home with no human contact in April. We were forced to work remotely from home as our "new normal" which caused stress and anxiety, and then surprisingly, I received a call in June, informing me that my position was being dissolved, and I was laid off from my job.

You talk about surprises (which I do not do well with). My entire world (literally) seems like it was crashing down. But, when I keep focusing on God's words, I am quickly reminded that I am a child of the Most-High God, and I am going to be okay. I keep telling myself that something good is going to come out of all of this. So, as hard as things may seem to be in your life, we all can take a look at our current situation through a different lens.

This book will help you identify your goals, and help you along the journey to achieve those goals. Even simple things in life are obtainable. You can quit smoking, overcome alcoholism or abuse, by following these simple but yet vital steps in achieving any goal you set out to achieve. All I ask is that you have a positive and relentless mindset as we embark on this journey together.

My seven steps to achieve your goals along with inspirational devotions will motivate you, not to only take your first step, but to cross the finish line!

Declare and decree this:

"I can do all things through Christ who strengthens me."

Philippians 4:13

Note to Self

**Trust Yourself.
You can do more
than you think.
You got this!**

GETTING STARTED

I always had dreams of writing a book. I will never forget the day that I visited a new doctor for an annual check-up over ten years ago, and she called me by my government name. I said, "Hi, but everyone calls me TK." She enthusiastically said, "TK! What does TK stand for?" I said, "It is the T and K from my government name (and she began to laugh)." And then, she quietly whispered, "TK! That name has a special ring to it; it sounds like a famous author's name, like J.K. Rowling or something." She then proceeded to ask me if I ever thought about becoming an Author? I looked at her and doubtfully replied, no. All I could focus on was getting through that awkward encounter of having my legs in stirrups while being questioned about my name.

But the truth be told, everything happens for a reason. For some odd reasons, that comment stayed with me for many years, and I always wondered if that was a sign from God. **Jesus says in John 4:48, "Unless you people see miraculous signs and wonders, you will never believe."** Let's just say I always thought about it, but never acted on it, until now.

As I write this book, I reflect on that moment, and I am so glad that I decided to follow my dreams of seeing my name listed as an Author (WOW, I did it, mom). The things people say or do to us can have an everlasting effect on us (good or bad), and it is up to us to act on it. I always say opportunities do not knock on your door, and then wait for you to open it; unless you were privileged enough to be born into a successful life. But for me, I had to work hard for everything I wanted. As my grandmother would say, you were not born with a silver spoon in your mouth, if you want something, go and get it! Nothing will ever happen until you act upon it. Taking the first step is simply getting started.

Even though I thought about becoming an author one day, it did not become an attainable goal for me until I wrote it down on my vision board in December 2019. Have you ever heard the saying, "don't talk about it; be about it"? There comes a time when we have to stop wishing and dreaming and take action. **The bible says in James 2:17, "*In the same way, faith by itself if it is not accompanied by action, is dead.*"** We have to be courageous enough to just do it.

No excuses, no perfect timing, when a person is ready, (and they are the only one that will know) they will do it. Someone can encourage you all day, provide you with all the resources you may need, but nothing will happen until YOU want to do it. Like I stated earlier, I always wanted to be an author, but year after year, I never ventured into it. It took me to lose my job and have nothing but time on my hands while being stuck in a house with four walls caving on me to finally move.

For days, I wondered, (here we go again) if God was trying to tell me something. So, I just asked him, God, what are you trying to tell me? And, if you would just listen long enough, HE will give you an answer. **Proverbs 3:5 says, "*Trust in the Lord with all your heart and lean not on your own understanding; in all thy ways, acknowledge Him, and He will direct your path.*"**

Sometimes, God closes doors, because he wants to place you on the path He designed for you. I truly believe that everything that happens to us (good or bad) was all a part of the plan. So, then I started to question God. I prayed for a six-figure salary and He blessed me with that job, why would the job be taken away? I was left confused and filled with anger. See, sometimes, we are not sure if it is the work of the Lord or the Devil. So, I asked for another sign (yes, I know, here we go again), I still was not convinced. I prayed to be in a high-level position, stacking my papers and working a job that was only a dream for me at some point. All of the daily demands, stress and anxiety turned into pure silence. And, just like that, my world came crashing down (I thought). Once again, I questioned my thoughts, could this really be God?

One day, I received a call from my cousin who wanted to know if I was going to attend her upcoming 50th birthday party and I had to break the bad news to inform her that I will not be attending. I was just not in the mood. I told her I just lost my job and did not feel like partying, so I turned our thirty-second call to an hour of a therapy session, and that's when she told me something that I already knew, but needed confirmation from God (okay God, this is the last time, I get it).

My cousin, who is a woman of God, and very

spiritual, began to tell me that everything happens for a reason. She began to say, "I truly believe God is trying to get your attention by slowing you down. I think you should use this time while you're not working and redirect your focus on being a motivational speaker." She began to tell me that God blessed me with a gift to inspire people and use this time to do so. She said the world needs healing right now and that I should allow God to use me for what He has designed me to be.

I just remember blacking out and drifting back into the conversation and simply told her, "thank you". There was my confirmation! I am going to take something bad and turn it into something good. No excuses, no pity parties. It was time to get started.

I share this story with you with the hopes to inspire you to listen to your inner-self. That talent, and skill-set that God has blessed you with, that business you would like to start…it is the time! It is time to take the necessary steps to turn your dreams into a reality, and ultimately make an income from it. They say if you choose a job you love, you will never have to work a day in your life. So, are you ready? Remember the goal is just to get started, you got this!

Declare and decree this:

"This is the day the Lord has made. I will rejoice and be glad in it."

Psalm 118:24

Note to Self

Today, decide to start and watch how your life will change.

ABOUT THE BOOK

A 7-Step Plan To Achieve Your Goals

Quite often, people ask me how I came up with my 7-steps to achieve goals. And, to be honest, these are simple principles that have helped people for centuries. Whenever I doubt to start a new venture that someone has already done, my husband is always reminding me that the bible says in **Ecclesiastes 1:9:** *"All things are wearisome, more than one can say. The eye never has enough of seeing, nor the ear its fill of hearing. What has been will be again, what has been done will be done again; there's nothing new under the sun."* In other words, there is nothing in the world that has not already happened, been seen, or been created; things exist now as they always have.

Keep this in mind, while you are waiting for the right moment to start. Trust me; I am a perfectionist, and the type of person that believes in waiting for the right time, and the right moment to move. But, I am here to tell you that while you are waiting, someone else is thinking of the same master plan, and inventing the next big thing while you're still waiting for the perfect moment. And, now you have lost out on a game-changing moment, trying to be a perfectionist. Yes, that person, the one that wants to keep trying over and over until they get it right.

Well, I have news for you, while you are taking your time introducing your plan to the world, Burger King is now selling tacos. Listen, I learned a long time ago that if you cannot beat them, join them. They are not the first fast-food chain to sell tacos, but they are the first burger joint that sells tacos. Now, let that sink in. You will never know if something will work for you until you try it.

I had the pleasure of researching and studying the world's most innovative leader, and pioneer of the personal computer revolution, Steve Jobs, to find out why Apple has been so successful. One of the things that I learned from Jobs is that he did not wait until he perfected a product, he would introduce it to the world, and if it did not work, he would simply start over or move to the next big thing.

He was not afraid to take a risk because he did not look at the setbacks as failures. Instead, he looked at them as learning opportunities. And, what he learned the most was something so simple; learn to think differently. Job's always said, "Simplicity is the new sophistication." Something so simple was the game-changer for Apple, and one of the reasons why they are still successful to this day. People always say think outside the box, but, who said that we had to go outside the box?

Instead, I challenge you to stay in the box and just think differently. Steve Jobs did not worry about the competitors. He just simply beat them to the punch of creating the next big thing. And, we all know that everyone wants to be the first, so keep this in mind when you are contemplating and waiting to move.

The seven steps that I will share with you was nothing that I invented. Instead, I just took motivational quotes and things that only life can teach you and came up with seven steps that worked for me. Everything that I am today is because of these simple steps that I took to achieve my goals. I truly believe we cannot just talk the talk, but we must walk the walk to know what works for us. And, if it worked for me, it could work for you.

Declare and decree this:

"I know the plans I have for you, declares the Lord, plans to prosper you and not to harm you, plans to give you hope and a future."

Jeremiah 29:11

Note to Self

Quit waiting for everything
to be perfect!
Don't say "there's
still time or maybe next time."
Because there's also
the concept of 'It's
too late!"

PLAN THE LIFE YOU WANT

STEP 1: KNOW WHAT YOU WANT

I believe, for you to go after anything in life, you must first know what you are aiming for. So, I must ask you, do you know what you want? Do you know where you are heading? If you don't know what you want, you end up with a lot of what you don't want (yes, take a minute to reflect on that, got it? good!). With that being said, be clear on what you want, and you will see how opportunities and solutions start appearing in your life. It is not magic. I am a firm believer that what we see, is what we are looking for, and the more we focus on the things we want; we have the power to achieve them.

Psalm 20:4 says, *"May He give you the desire of your heart and make all your plans succeed."* God has the power to answer all of our prayers, but before you prayed, you knew exactly what you wanted God to help you with. It is very seldom, that someone will turn to

God and not know what they are praying for. The same thing applies to your goals and the things you want out of life.

I knew at a very young age that I wanted to become a professional dancer, and I enjoyed entertaining people. But, I also knew, that where I came from, we did not have the money for me to take professional dance lessons, so for years, I had to teach myself how to dance if I wanted to become an amazing dancer and travel the world. Like I stated earlier, I was not born with a silver spoon in my mouth, and had to work hard for everything I wanted out of life.

At the tender age of ten, I began to mock Michael and Janet Jackson. I entered into local talent shows and would blow people's socks off. I knew then that God blessed me with a gift, and I saw that as a way to get out of the hood. While my friends were hanging out at the local park, I was constantly in front of the television, watching music videos, and learning all of the choreography and moves from my favorite celebrities. I taught myself how to dance, and because

I was passionate about it, dance became my life. So much so, after years of dancing in both the NFL and

NBA, and ultimately travelling around the world as a back-up dancer for many videos, and major recording artist, I decided to open my dance studio and give back to my community.

I wanted to inspire children just like me, who had dreams of becoming a dancer but could not afford professional lessons. I offered scholarships to the under-deserved to give them hope and wanted them to look at me as a constant reminder that their upbringing does not determine their future. It is not where you are born, but where you are going that counts. Many of the children that took dance lessons under my direction have gone on to do some amazing and exceptional things in the dance world. I am glad that I played a part in helping them to fulfill many of their dreams.

But, imagine if I didn't know what I wanted? Or what if I didn't know what I wanted to accomplish? I often wonder where would I be or what will I be doing if I didn't have dreams and knew what I wanted out of life.

Therefore, I encourage you to think about your goals and know what you would like to accomplish. People often go through life just living day by day with no purpose or ambition. I am not here to say anything is wrong with that, if that is how people choose to live their life, it is their prerogative. But, when you live a life with dreams and goals that you want to accomplish, I believe that you can create a more meaningful and purposeful life that God uniquely designed you to live. The bible says in **Philippians 4:19:** *"And this same God who takes care of me will supply all your needs from his glorious riches, which have been given to us in Christ Jesus."*

It Is Okay To Change Courses

I am not the one that will go through life, thinking everything is going to be perfect. Just as you will encounter blessings and advancements, you will also come across unexpected setbacks and challenges. My advice to you will be to keep your eyes on the prize. If the plan does not work, change the plan but never change the goal. **2 Corinthians 4:8 says,** *"We are afflicted in every way, but not crushed; perplexed, but not driven to despair; persecuted, but not forsaken; struck down, but not destroyed."* For example, you are going to have many different goals along the way. Some you may achieve and others you may not. Some will change, because life itself is always changing and it is okay if you change courses. I have started many new ventures of what success looks like to me.

I went back to school to become a broadcast journalist, and I accomplished that dream of graduating from the program and taking an internship with a local news station in Miami.

Despite me taking a few reporting gigs here and there, I knew for me to become the mega TV reporter that I desired to be, I eventually needed to move to a city that will ultimately work in my favor. I had thoughts of moving to Los Angles and Atlanta where I knew I could be recognized as a talented and well-rounded on-air reporter, hosting my own talk show. Because of this dream, I set up goals for myself to go back to school and study broadcast television. And, I did just that; I graduated the top of my class and was recognized as the Best All-Around Student. After my internship, I landed an on-air job as a local sports reporter, interviewing top high school and professional athletes across Miami. It was the start of something big (I thought).

But, during this time, (unexpectedly) I ran into a

former high school classmate at an event and things took a different turn. I have not seen this guy in over 20 years, and there he was in a police uniform (heyyyyy Mr. Officer) staring at me and for some reason, this tickling feeling came over me. Wait, why does he look so good? This is not the same kid from high school (Lord, Jesus take the wheel). And, just like that, we locked eyes, had a brief conversation, exchanged numbers and went on a date that night, and the rest is history. Yes, I fell in love, and my plan changed. How so TK? Glad you asked.

See, I chose love over chasing one of my dreams. I knew if I moved to LA or Atlanta, my chances of trying to make it work with him would be slim to none. I was at a cross-road of choosing love or career. So, I chose love. It was something that my heart desired, and I prayed for. And, I am so glad that I chose love because that fine officer and I got married and I am living out a dream, but it is a different dream.

You have to remember, that things will happen in life that we do not prepare for, but we have to be willing to stop, pause, take a deep breath and strategically change the course. See, I did not give up on my dreams;

I just changed the plan of becoming a TV reporter to a six-figure business-woman by day and started my own consulting business as a side hustle by night. Sometimes, things happen for a reason. You may not understand at that present time, but it will all make sense later.

This book is a prime example of unexpected blessings. You talk about surprises, the year 2020 has been nothing but unexpected setbacks. I just want to throw the entire year away! But, I decided to change my mindset, and focus on the big picture.

I can both succumb to depression and sorrow about losing my job while going through one of the most challenging years ever. Or I can utilize this time, to focus on my speaking business and write my book. I even shared my thoughts and disappointment with my coach, and he encouraged me to write during this time. I will share with you what he told me. He said, "Our best work comes from our adversities. It is easy to write when everything is going well. But, imagine you sharing your story of how you overcame your struggles with the world; ultimately inspiring someone to do the same. Now, that is victory!"

There's an old saying, "If life serves you lemons, make lemonade." Well, I say, "If life serves you lemons, pass me the salt and tequila!" Yes, setbacks, challenges and adversities will come. Maybe you relapsed or got a divorce, had a tragic loss or a pandemic came and rocked the entire universe. Regardless of what challenge you are facing right now, know that this too shall pass.

During these times, do what you can and ask for help if needed. Put things into perspective and take care of yourself. Find ways to discover self-love and focus on your mental health. Replenish your energy and strengthen your faith and draw yourself closer to God. But, whatever you do, DO NOT GIVE UP!

Declare and decree this:

"What I decide on will be done, and light will shine on my ways."

Job 22:28

Note to Self

If you don't go after what you want, you'll never have it!

PLAN THE LIFE YOU WANT

STEP 2: SET YOUR GOALS

Goals help us become better versions of ourselves. I believe when you write your goals down, it means that you can visually see them, and they become obtainable. It is extremely important because when we see something, it affects how we act. You are more likely to be more productive when you know what you are aiming for instead of just thinking or dreaming about it. This is a practice that I preach. This is not what I heard, but what I know to be true, and I believe in the power of attraction. What we manifest and focus on comes to fruition.

I know it seems cliché and only those who believe in the power of attraction will understand. Have you ever thought about your dream car and wonder why you see the exact car of your dreams (make, model and color) every time you go out on the road? Folks, this is called the power of attraction. It is the attractive and magnetic power of the universe that manifests through everyone and everything. Have you ever noticed that what we focus on becomes our thoughts? And if they become our thoughts, they can become our reality.

Proverbs 18:21 says, "*The tongue has the power of life and death.*" Your words can either speak life or death. Our tongues can build others up, or tear them down. If you continue to tell yourself that you are not worthy and feel ugly, you will feel exactly that way, and you can invite people to your pity-party. Or you have the choice to tell yourself that you are beautiful and continuously tell yourself that you are loved, you will feel that way. The choice is yours; change your words, and see your life change. I always say, from my mouth to God's ears after each prayer. So, go right ahead and tell Him what you want.

To be quite honest, what will it hurt to write your goals down on paper (date it) and put it away in a safe place? And, every, now and then check on your progress. The steps that I share with you are not steps I inherited from strangers, these are steps that I personally took, and they worked for me.

Personal Testimony: Back on November 10, 2014, I wrote all my goals and heart desires down on paper and placed the sheet in my Bible, under the book of Nehemiah. Three years later, when I was going through my Bible, the sheet fell out, that was when I discovered the meaning of manifestation. I could not believe it, everything that I wrote down happened. I had earned a six-figure salary, I became an on-air reporter, I had a better relationship with my family, and I got married to the man of my dreams.

Surprisingly, I had to share the good news with someone, because people would not believe me from just talking. So, I shared my goals with my husband as I began to cry. Tears began to roll down my face because I knew the pain and hurt that I had to endure to get to that point.

I know the desires that I mentioned seems obtainable and easy to others, but when you have gone through struggles of growing up in poverty and have endured a painful divorce that left you and your children with scars, you would never understand the hope I felt in that very moment.

See, it was only a dream for me to earn a six-figure

salary because I have never made that type of money before. And, to be quite honest, no other woman in my family has made that type of money, so it is hard to see women of color achieve such a goal.

As productive citizens, we go through life hearing how we need to get an education, give 110% in everything we do and strive for excellence but when an employee has to overcome obstacles and beat the odds, to achieve all of those accomplishments despite her conditions, the color of her skin, gender and upbringing, it makes the opportunity to land a leadership role within a major organization that much rewarding and sweeter.

Before I was allowed to work as the only Black Leader in a huge healthcare system, my mother and grandmother both worked for the same organization for over 35 years.

My grandmother was a cafeteria worker for 38 years and never advanced to a leadership role and was ultimately laid off after four decades of service. My mother worked clerical jobs in administration for the same company for 29 years with no advancements until she recently retired in 2019. My aunt and cousin have worked for the same company for decades. As you can see, being part of this organization for so many years was an honor in my family. So, when they heard the great news that I secured a leadership role with the same organization, they were extremely proud of me. They wanted to see me achieve something that was not a reality to them.

However, that reward did not come easy! It is much harder for blacks (and especially women of color) to move up the ladder and be given the same opportunities to lead a major organization. I sacrificed as a single mother to take out loans to go back to school to achieve my Bachelor's degree and pushed myself to obtain my Master's degree four years later. I did not stop there; I decided that I would go back to school to get a broadcast and journalism degree. I knew if I wanted to become a top executive one day, I would need the credentials to secure a seat at the table with other leaders. I invested in my professional development and proudly have worked in the non-profit sector for over 15 years, so, I came with a lot of experience as a fundraiser.

Achieving this goal was truly a game-changer for me. I needed my children to see that if they work hard, they can achieve anything they set their mind to achieve, and not allow racial equity and equality ruin opportunities for them. I wanted them to learn to continue to fight the good fight and go after what they want.

And, for the love and marriage thing (oh yeah)… until you have been through a bitter divorce that literally cost you everything and you hit rock bottom, you will never know the love and desire to trust someone again. I became scared to love again and was afraid to open up to anyone who got too close to me. I became shielded and overly protective of my children to keep all of us away from hurt and pain. A bitter divorce is a dark and hurtful place to be, and I do not wish it on my worst enemy. The embarrassment, the shame, the anger, and hopelessness, I think I went through all the stages of grief from a tragic loss.

And, as a mother, it is devastating to watch what a divorce can do to your children and family. I was broken and wounded. So, for me to find love again is a huge accomplishment. That is why I always say be kind to people. You just never know what they are going through. That was a battle that I had to overcome and if it was not for the grace of God, I would have crumbled. See, adversities come to make us stronger and I do not see my divorce as a failure but as a lesson. Sometimes, we cannot go back and change anything that happened, but we can definitely change the outcome. I refused to lose and allow myself to stay down. Therefore, do not have any regrets or sorrow of your past, but to thank the Lord for second chances. Won't He Do It!

Hitting rock bottom led me to God. I was in so much pain that I cried out to Him. And, I know it was nothing but the grace of God that protected and healed me from my scars. Until you have an intimate relationship with God, you cannot learn how to trust and love yourself and others.

This is why putting goals down on paper became such a pivotal point in my life. Things that I never thought would happen, all of sudden became real. Of course, I had to take the necessary steps and apply myself to doing the work that was needed, but at least I had a vision of what I wanted and built up enough courage to go after it.

Because of this aha moment, I hosted my first vision board party to inspire others to do the same. During that event, women laughed and cried together, and more importantly, we empowered each other. Please keep in mind that your goals may not always be good habits, but we all have room for improvement to get rid of a few bad habits as well.

Battling addiction, depression or a mental illness is not easy. But, we must take little small steps to move towards victory. Please remember that during this journey, we must even celebrate the small victories and encourage one another.

Assignment: Therefore, I challenge you today to create your vision board and place it somewhere visible as a constant reminder or write down your goals (do not forget the date) on paper and place it in a sacred place (you will thank me later).

Declare and Decree this:

"I will write down the revelation and make it plain on tablets so that a herald may run with it."

Habakkuk 2:2

Note to Self

"Write it down on paper with a real pencil. And watch sh** get real."

— Erykah Badu —

PLAN THE LIFE YOU WANT

STEP 3: CREATE A PLAN

Once you have written down your goals, now it is time to think of an action plan. The first mistake people make when achieving their goals, is to live in a fantasy world, daydreaming all day about their desires, and thinking they are going to magically appear. If no one has ever told you before, let me be the first to inform you that dreams and accomplishments do not come knocking at your door; you have to put in the work to obtain the goals. And, the best way to be effective and productive during this process is to create a plan with realistic steps to achieve the goal.

Having a strategic plan will provide you with clear direction and create accountability that will keep you on task and help you get to the finish line. Let us think about this for a minute, how can you reach for the stars and the moon, if you do not have a road map or plan to show you how to get there?

Before you were even born, God designed a plan for your life **(Jeremiah 29:11)**. He knows the beginning and the end of our story. If God can take the time to create an individual plan for our lives, we can take the necessary steps to carry out the dreams and aspirations that He has instilled in us.

Let's Talk Business

Planning is not only an essential process in our personal lives, but it is also a substantial tool that is used to identify goals within businesses. Preparing for the future allows business leaders to consider the impact they would like the company to have and to find a way to get there. It is even beneficial for teams within an organization to set clear and attainable goals together so everyone can be on the same page and work in unison towards a common purpose.

Creating a plan also allows you to prioritize the steps and more importantly, think about what will work and what will not work. It is an opportunity to identify and prepare for any possible threats and unusual circumstances. For example, the entire nation is in the middle of a financial crisis from the effects of the Coronavirus.

Many businesses have been left with so much uncertainty for the future, which has caused many of them to shut down, and go out of business. I'm quite sure many companies did not have a recovery plan in place that will prepare them for such an unprecedented circumstance that will forever change the way we do business. Even though we may have a step-by-step plan in place, you would still need to be prepared for any unexpected situations that may occur. Preparing for any unexpected turbulence is a smart tactic that applies to both our personal and professional well-being.

The legendary Prince, said it best, "Dearly beloved, we have gathered here today to get through this thing called life." If you have not gone through any hardship or challenging times; and in the words of my late great grandmother, Mary Crawford, "keep on living!"

Spiritual Advice: During the challenging times, remain on course and do not take your focus off the big picture. We can plan, but we also need to trust God and know that He will guide us in our paths. Ask Him to guide your footsteps and trust the process. **Isaiah 41:10 says, *"So do not fear, for I am with you; do not be dismayed, for I am your God. I will strengthen you***

and help you; I will hold you with my righteous right hand." Creating a plan to achieve your goals is only a method that will make your journey easier, by keeping you on target. When you fall off, you have the power to get back up and continue along the path of success.

Assignment: I challenge you to set goals for the things you would like to achieve or accomplish. Identify and prioritize your steps and keep them in a visible place to help you stay focused. It is also good to share your plan with a close relative or friend so they can hold you accountable and cheer you on along the way.

Declare and Decree this:

"I will plan my course, but will ask God to establish my steps."

Proverbs 16:9

PLAN THE LIFE YOU WANT

STEP 4: TAKE ACTION

Walt Disney once said, "The way to get started is to quit talking and begin doing." Now that you have written your plan, it is time to take action! I'm still amazed at people who set goals for themselves and think they are going to happen just because they made a wish or said a prayer. As stated earlier in **James 2:17, "*In the same way, faith by itself, if it is not accompanied by action, is dead.*"** It is not wise to set a goal and not take the necessary steps to achieve that goal. Creating a plan will help you identify what you should be working towards and what steps to take to ultimately move you in the right direction to make your dreams come true.

For example, if going back to school or graduating with a college degree is a personal goal of yours, there are a few steps that need to be identified for you to achieve that goal:

1) **Decide** what college you would like to attend

2) **Choose** a major

3) **Research** the admission qualifications for this school.

4) **Apply** to your school of choice

5) **Speak** to a Financial Aid and Academic Advisor

6) **Create** a plan and select courses needed for your major

7) **Finish** all your assignments, study, and receive good grades

8) **Complete** all the required courses and requirements

9) **Prepare** for graduation

10) **Walk** across that stage and receive your diploma!

Did you notice anything in particular with the above list? I purposely selected action words that place accountability on you taking action to obtain each step. See, you cannot talk about going back to school without taking those simple steps to make it happen. Without taking action, your reality of achieving your dreams and goals becomes more difficult. I am not saying that you cannot accomplish your goals without a plan, but why work harder when you can work smarter? Let us get back to the basics of following instructions, which is why they were created in the first place; to make things easier to follow.

It takes a lot of Courage to Move!

This step is probably one of the most important, yet the hardest to carry out. Let us think about it. We know exactly what needs to be done, but in our minds, we give ourselves a thousand and one excuses not to start. It takes courage to finally say, enough is enough. I will start today (and mean it). Taking that first step towards your victory is rewarding in itself. All we have to do is move and celebrate the small victories along the way. The fact that you finally "did" (action word) something about it is a game-changer and do NOT allow anyone to discourage you from believing in yourself.

The mind is a powerful communicator and has the ability to control everything we do, including taking action. Once we have made up our minds to do something, we can conquer anything we set our minds to accomplish.

The Bible says in **Matthew 21:22:** *"whatever you ask in prayer, you will receive, if you have faith."*

A year ago, I had the pleasure of being the keynote speaker at a graduation ceremony. Leading up to the graduation day, I was contemplating what message I wanted to leave with the students. I will never forget that my husband and I went to the movies to watch the remake of Disney's "The Lion King" (oh, how I wish we can go to the movies again, but oh no, we're locked in the house in quarantine). Sorry, I had a moment, now back to what I was saying.

When I was watching the movie, The Lion King, I noticed at the beginning of the film, all of the animals in the jungle ran to Pride Rock so they can have the first glance of the King's son. But, what I was more amazed at was the fact that every animal in the jungle had so much respect for Mufasa and kneeled out of respect once he appeared at the edge of the rock. It was amazing! And, then it hit me, why do they have so much respect for Mufusa?

Why is the lion considered the King of the jungle?

Yes, I know...why am I thinking so deep, right? But, seriously, what is it about the lion that demands respect from the other animals? He is not the tallest animal, that is the giraffe. He is not the strongest animal, that is probably a rhinoceros. He is not the fastest, that is a cheetah. So, what is it about the lion that makes the other animals bow down?

Let us think about the play, The Wizard of Oz. What did the lion want from the Great Oz? Courage! And, that was when it hit me, it is because the lion is the most courageous animal of them all. He has no fear and will challenge any animal in the jungle to claim his throne! I know that's why Disney selected Beyonce' to play Nala because she is Queen Bey! Okay, okay, I keep getting side-tracked. But do you get my point?

Having enough courage to move is all you need to begin your journey. And, I promise you, once you have made up your mind that you are ready, the process gets simpler. Like I said earlier, getting started is the hardest, and most courageous part of fulfilling our dreams. But, just know that it will all be worth it. So, if you need to tap into your inner Mufasa and Simba, let me be the first to cheer you on! So, go and be Courageous! You Got This...Hakuna Matata!

Assignment: Once you have written down your goals, I want you to write down any fears you may be experiencing that could possibly hold you back from getting started. Read those fears out loud and then repeat after me: **"Today, I have decided that this is the day that I will conquer my fears!"** Now, repeat it three times and say it like you mean it!

Declare and Decree this:

"God didn't give us a spirit of fear but of power, love and of a sound mind."

2 Timothy 1:7

PLAN THE LIFE YOU WANT

Note to Self

Thinking will not overcome fear but ACTION will. Go get it!

PLAN THE LIFE YOU WANT

STEP 5: BE READY!

I was always taught that if you stay ready, you will never have to get ready. There is nothing worse than having someone offer you a job, and you did not prepare yourself for it. It will be a missed opportunity. If you pray for something, you have to be ready to receive it! How can you ask for a dream job, and have not taken the time to invest in that field? I believe in prioritizing your goals and start doing the necessary steps to achieve those goals, and then (in some cases) wait patiently for an opportunity or right moment to walk into your purpose.

Be prepared, whether the time is favorable or not. Sometimes, we have to continue doing the things we less desire until we receive that promotion or that dream job. You must become a master in that field, learn everything you need to know about that particular skill and prepare yourself with everything you need to achieve what you are trying to obtain. And, even when you have achieved that degree in that field or have the work experience needed to land the job, there is always an opportunity to improve your personal and professional development while waiting.

Here are a few steps you can do to prepare yourself for what you desire:

1) You can expand your knowledge and take a course about your goal

2) Take online webinars

3) You can research or order books on a particular topic

4) Find a mentor or coach

5) Seek counseling (if needed)

6) Get involved with a support group or connect with like-minded people

7) Contact Coach TK (smiles)

Matthew 24:44 says, "So you also must be ready, because the Son of Man will come at an hour when you do not expect him." In other words, we were all designed with a purpose here on earth, and I will challenge you and ask, are you fulfilling the life that God has planned for you? Are you preparing yourself for His return and will He be pleased with you? Please remember that it is never too late to fix our lives or work on something that you know will be better for your life.

Maybe it is a health issue. Perhaps you need to eat healthier or lose weight. Whatever challenges you would like to overcome or achievements you will want to accomplish, know that you have the power to do it! If you desire to lose weight, you will have to prepare yourself for your weight loss journey. You would not only work on your physical endurance, but you will have to work on your mental stability to remain focused on your goal to lose the desired weight. *"Before anything else, preparation is the key to success." - Alexander Graham Bell*

So, if you have not started, get ready! Because everything you desire might just become your reality sooner than you think. And, as you prepare yourself, please know that nothing is ever given to you in life; you will have to earn it (unless you were born into wealth). But, I am referring to the general population that has to work hard to get ahead. I often hear people wish others good luck when they would like to see you accomplish something.

However, I prefer not to use the word luck because luck does not produce any results. A wise man once told me (that wise man is my intelligent and fine husband) that luck is merely a crossroad where preparation meets opportunity! Therefore, prepare yourself, so you will be ready to walk into your purpose when someone opens the door of opportunity! To put things into perspective, no job, degree, or a car will just magically show up at your doorstep. You will have to go out and work hard to earn it. Please always remember that you get what you work for. So, instead of wishing you luck, I will say "Go Get It!"

Now on a side note, if things just miraculously happen to you, please do not get luck and God's favor mixed up. He is the only one that can show that type of favor over your life and bless you when you have not done one single thing to deserve it, and I will rather give Him all the credit and praise for such blessings.

Declare and Decree this:

"Therefore, I will prepare my mind for action, keep sober in spirit, fix my hope completely on the grace to be brought to me at the revelation of Jesus Christ."

1 Peter 1:13

Note to Self

"By failing to prepare, you are preparing to fail."
— Benjamin Franklin —

PLAN THE LIFE YOU WANT

STEP 6: DON'T GIVE UP

This chapter resonates well with me right now. I really can find a thousand reasons why I am unable to complete this book after all of the challenges that 2020 has thrown at me these past few months. But, I am determined to finish. I have to make the best out of my current situation and constantly motivate myself some days to write even when I don't feel like getting out of bed (like today). There are some days that I feel like these four walls are caving in on me, after being locked up in the house for months due to the pandemic, and also losing my job.

The one thing the pandemic has taught me was to take care of myself. For so long, I was always everyone else's cheerleader and support system. I always put others before myself. I constantly find myself asking, who motivates the motivator? I have learned that I cannot fill up someone else's cup when my cup is empty! I have gained a newfound respect for self-love and self-care and what matters the most. And, that is to take care of me first. You cannot care for anyone else until you learn how to care for yourself first.

During these challenging times, I have found a way to create a healthy lifestyle for myself by establishing a weekly routine. I make sure that I work out at least 3 to 4 times a week (mainly outdoor activities to change the atmosphere). And, I discovered that it is the little things that mean the most when you are facing obstacles. I never knew the personal gratification of riding a bike outside or what taking a jog on the beach will do for your mental health. Just having the freedom to walk outside, and listen to the birds became therapeutic to me.

During challenging times, you really learn to appreciate life. It all starts with having the right mindset and remaining positive through it all. Always remember to keep your eyes on the prize. That is one of the reasons why I am so adamant about setting goals. Can you imagine if I was going through hard times without anything to focus on? At that point, you are just living day to day with no direction. I literally will go insane if I did not have goals and objectives for my life. Whew

Jesus, just take the wheel!

I say all of that to say this, I have a thousand reasons why I should not be able to write this book, but I refuse to give up! Is it easy? No, it is not easy when everything around you feels like it is falling apart. At this very moment, thousands of people are dying every day from the virus, and some days I feel like a failure because my marriage is facing problems, and I am not currently working. And, as if that is not enough, I'm also the caregiver for my mother and grandmother and would like to add that 2020 is the first of many times that I don't have my father here with me. My first father's day without him, his first birthday without him and now the holidays are quickly approaching.

Trust me, I can succumb to everything I'm going through, but I refuse to lose. My grandma always told me that troubles don't last always, and I know that better days are coming. **1 Peter 5:10 says, *"Be patient, God has an eternity of better days. Do his will on earth with joy and await your reward."*** Having faith in the Lord is what keeps me going. So, don't you dare give up! Please remember that you can do all things through Christ (**Philippians 4:13**).

If we were taught to quit every time something became hard, we would not know that little kid from North Carolina named Michael Jordan. Did you know that he was cut from the Varsity Basketball team in high school? Imagine the rejection he must have felt after trying out for the team and giving it his all and was notified that he did not make the team. That rejection could have left him scarred, and he could have given up on basketball. Instead, he took the feedback his coach gave him and practiced every day to become one of the best players that graduated from his high school. And ultimately, became one of the best basketball players in the world and the rest is history.

Did you know that Steve Jobs (who I admire) was fired from Apple before he became the face of Apple and changed the evolution of technology and how it is used today? Jobs have stated several times, that being fired from Apple was the best thing that ever happened to him. He felt that heaviness of his success was replaced by the lightness of being able to begin again. It was at his "reset era" that he was at his most creative self and started two new companies named NeXT and Pixar. Pixar would go on to become the most successful animation studio that was bought out by Apple, which eventually brought Jobs back to Apple. Imagine if he had given up?

Did you know that Beyonce' was cut from a television show called Star Search (Lord, I'm showing my age) looking for the next big star? Boy, did those judges get that wrong? Beyonce' is now one of the world's biggest stars and is considered one of the best entertainers of all times! Do I need to say more? Can you imagine if she had quit singing after that? She was only ten years old and had to deal with such rejection on live TV. And, for the record, since this is my book, I would just like to throw in that I'm the biggest Beyonce' fan, so I had to find a way to mention her name (I'm just saying, respect Queen Bey). OK, carry on!

Do you think successful people do not have problems? Well, if you have not been told, let me be the first to tell you that they have more problems than most people. Notorious BIG said it best, "Mo' Money, Mo' Problems!" Please do not think that money will buy you happiness. Do I need to remind you that I am currently unemployed and have found more joy in riding my bike in my neighborhood listening to 90's R&B music than I have ever been? As the beautiful and late singer Aaliyah once said, "At first you don't succeed, dust yourself off and try again."

If you are going through hard times, please know that you are not alone. We all face hard times, and it is fine to take a break or even detour if necessary, but never give up on the dreams and goals that you have set for yourself. Remember to surround yourself with people who will motivate you! And, when all fails, please remember that you have to become your biggest cheerleader and motivate yourself. Until things getter better (and they will if you believe) take this time to do the things you love to do and redirect your focus on the things that are important to you.

Declare and Decree this:

"I will not become weary in doing good, for at the proper time, I will reap a harvest if I do not give up."

Galatians 6:9

PLAN THE LIFE YOU WANT

Step #7

Be You!

STEP 7: BE YOU!

Oh, how I strategically saved this step for the last! If you don't know by now, the number seven is me and my husband's favorite number. The number seven means completion and perfection (both physical and spiritual). It derives much of its meaning from being tied directly to God's creation of all things. We were married during the 7th month of the year on the 7th day during 2017. I had seven bridesmaids, and he had seven groomsmen, and we complete one another. So, I saved step seven as my last and most important message to you. If you do not remember any of the steps I have shared with you, please remember this message: In all that you do, please remember to BE YOU, unapologetically YOU!

Be who God called you to be and stay true to who you are. There is nothing worse than living a lie and pretending to be something that you are not. And, trust me, I get it, we want people to like us, so we put up a fake facade to feel better about ourselves. But, the reality and most important thing to learn from life are to be your authentic self and those who are meant to love you will adjust and accept you the way you are. Quit trying to please people and live the life that you want to live and be who you want to be.

The bible says in John 8:32, *"Then you will know the truth, and the truth will set you free."*

Even on our jobs, we are told how to act and what to do, but when following the laws and bylaws, still know that your personality is YOUR personal characteristic that makes you uniquely you. Please don't try to be Susan from across the hallway, be you and people will still love you.

I realized I was very different growing up, when everyone wanted to go left, I went right. I have never really wanted to be like anyone (Ok, except for Janet Jackson or Beyonce'). But you get my point. Even when I tried out for the Miami HEAT Dancers, I did not fit the desired image they were looking for. Back in the '90s, they were looking for the girl next door, long hair, beauty. And, I remember walking into the auditions with a bold short haircut and an attitude (not a stuck-up or nasty attitude). But, an attitude like *"who gon' check me boo!"* Let us say that I made the dance team and was bold enough to change the narrative about women and how we are supposed to look or carry ourselves.

That was when I discovered that it is okay to be different. Wait, let me rephrase that, it is indispensable to be different. So, I dare you to be different! Yes, I am called extra, but extraordinary people are meant to be nothing more or nothing less than themselves. I never denied it or tried to change who I am, I just simply accepted it. I have accepted my flaws, scars and personal dislikes and decided that I am who I am. Over the years, life as a way of molding us to be who we are designed to be. Now, I'm not telling you to go live a hateful and deceitful life and accept it, I am clearly stating that life is about choices. And, it is your life, and you can choose your path, if that is the type of life you want, that is you.

I just chose to live a positive and caring life. I truly believe what you put out into the universe, is what you will receive back. And, I have nothing but love to give.

So, if someone is going to love you, shouldn't they know the real you? Let them decide if you are the right fit for them, and you have the right to pick what is best for you. That includes people, places, jobs, everything around you. Feel free to design your life and your path to your own happiness.

I learned from my mentor a long time ago, that not everyone is going to like you. I left that meeting, confused and shocked. What do you mean everyone is not going to like me? I could not accept that some people would not like me when I'm so nice, and loving to everyone. Whew chile, the accuracy of accepting the truth. I found out it does not matter how loving you are or how pure your intentions may be, people are who they are, and everyone is not you! They don't think like you or live a positive life like you; and like Bobby Brown said, "it is their prerogative". Some people really hate that I'm so happy all the time, my personality probably annoys them. But, it is okay, I will rather be happy and annoying than miserable and hateful.

I have learned that I get to choose the narrative of my life, and you can do the same. Don't you dare be sorry for being you! Being your true self will help make your journey of achieving your goals easier as you navigate through the ups and the down of life. At least you are being authentic and true to your choices. And, believe it or not, people may not like you, but they will respect you. And, if they don't, you have the power to dismiss them or dismiss yourself from anyone who cannot accept you the way you are. So, stop trying to fit in or be like someone else. God took his time and designed us so different that no one on this earth has the same fingerprints or DNA as you. So, why in the..... (that was close, I almost curse) do you want to be like someone else?

That is why I'm really concerned about the pressure this generation is facing due to social media influence. Nowadays, it is about the number of likes and complimentary comments that feeds their soul. Social media is just like everything else in this world, it has its good and bad features. It is good because you get to stay connected to your loved ones and know what is going on around the world in a split of an eye. And, the negative side is that some people (not all) hide behind the truth.

They are living a lie and posting things that are not

true just so people will like them. I will be the first to tell you; please do not get caught up into what people post on social media and compare it to your life. Everyone will have seasons of ups and downs, and you have to remember that people may not (including me) post their troubles or downfalls on their social media platforms. So, be happy for people and keep it moving.

There is no need to be like them, remain true to you and know that your season of joy is coming too. Social media is a powerful tool, so choose your message and what you would like to be known for. That is why I made a decision a long time ago, that I will use my platform to promote love, family and joyful things. We have enough negativity going on in the world that I choose to pour out positive vibes! OMG, I literally can write a book on this topic alone. I'm extremely passionate about people being happy and the first step in being truly happy is being happy with who you are.

Being true to yourself will ultimately help you when you are trying to select goals and aspirations that are best for you. You can be happy with the choices you made and know that you have the power to tackle your goals the way you wanted to. Do not give someone else that much power over your life to tell you what you can or cannot do or be. And, as my mentor told me, I will tell you, "not everyone is going to like you" but who cares? Live your life for you and do what makes you happy. Period!

Declare and Decree this:

"I praise you because I am fearfully and wonderfully made; your works are wonderful, I know that full well."

Psalm 139:14

Note to Self

"Be yourself; everyone else is already taken."

– Oscar Wilde –

WRAPPING UP

As we come to an end, I hope I was able to shed some light on the matter and offer guidance in helping you achieve your goals. The steps that I have provided are not something I heard, but it was actual life lessons that helped me along the way. I believe that we all can learn from one another without any judgment or condescending feelings. No one here on earth is perfect, and things may not go as planned, but I'm a true believer that setting goals and creating plans can make things easier as we navigate through this thing call life. I tell people all the time, let us work smarter not harder.

So, when life throws you a curveball, you will still be able to knock the ball out of the ballpark because you will adjust accordingly. I will rather live my life knowing exactly what I want for myself, and setting goals to achieve the things I want, creates accountability for my actions and keeps me on a straight path. So, when something does not go right (or my way) I cannot and will not blame anyone else. We have to realize that we are 100% responsible for the decisions we make and the life we choose, so choose wisely. Goals are what make us move closer to our dreams.

They are the first steps towards victory of what we want to achieve, and you must realize the significance of setting goals. Applying these simple steps will help you measure your progress, and when you see the results, it will motivate you to do more. Victory is achieving whatever goal you would like to achieve (big or small). And, once you truly believe in your ability to do it, you can achieve anything. It all starts with having a positive attitude and creating a determined spirit that will overcome any obstacle that may come your way.

I know it sounds cliché, but Walt Disney did not become successful by making up quotes that he did not believe. He became successful because he dared to dream the imaginable and wanted to share his formula of success with the world. I dare you to do the same. If you end up setting goals for yourself from this reading, I would love to hear about your achievements. I hope I was able to inspire you with my personal testimonies and offer you some hope towards anything you are facing.

You wouldn't believe the comfort this book as brought me during this difficult time in my life. It is still surreal to know that it was just a dream that I would become an author one day. And, now I can finally check this accomplishment off my vision board and add the title Author to my biography. And, with your help, hopefully, one day I will be a Best Selling Author.

I will be honest to tell you that I don't like writing, (I love to talk, can't you tell) and for years I would put off writing a book because of an insecure trait thinking I would not be successful at it. But, look at me now! I have truly learned that everything happens for a reason, even during a storm, you can find the good. If I was never laid off from my job, I probably would not have ever found the time to write my first book. Only God knows where this journey will lead me, and I will continue to trust him along this journey wholeheartedly. I believe and want the same for the person reading this book.

Please remember that you can do anything you set your mind to do. I pray that you accomplish all of your dreams and goals and know with will and determination, they are achievable.

Declare and Decree this:

"May God give me the desire of my heart and make all of my plans succeed."

Psalm 20:4

PLAN THE LIFE YOU WANT

Note to Self

"If you can dream it,
you can do it!"
– Walt Disney –

ABOUT THE AUTHOR

Professionally, TK serves as the Founder and CEO of TKO Consulting LLC, where she provides speaking, coaching and training services. As a speaker and success coach, TK is a proud certified team member of the author, speaker and pastor, John Maxwell and a proud board member of the Ladies of Success Entrepreneur Women's group led by the reality star, Nene Leakes.

Educationally, TK has a Bachelor's degree in Business Administration, a Master's in Leadership and she is a certified Broadcast Journalist. She has served as an entertainment reporter and reported on local entertainment news, celebrity gossip, social events, and an array of music festivals, such as Jazz in the Gardens and the Overtown Music Festival. TK has been a professional dancer for both the NFL and NBA and is known and respected as a professional choreographer for over 20 years.

Through all of her accomplishments and achievements, modestly, TK wants to be known for her positive spirit and kind heart. So much so, that TK inspires to become an internationally known motivational speaker to help others learn how to live a positive and purposeful life. Her most recent accomplishment was becoming an Author and writing her first book, **Plan The Life You Want** to help people achieve their goals and dreams.

Personally, TK was born and raised in Miami, FL. She is married to a Lieutenant with Miami-Dade Police Department and is a proud mom of two beautiful adult children and step-mom to two handsome boys. Her favorite book is *The Power of Positive Thinking* by Norman Vincent Peale and her favorite quote is *"Be yourself; everyone else is already taken."* by Oscar Wilde.

She loves to dance in her spare time and is a positive, energetic and loving person with a "larger than life" personality.

TESTIMONIALS

"TK's energy and spirit are infectious. It's impossible to forget her or to leave a room she is in and not feel more inspired and grateful." – **Karen**

"TK is very inspirational and empowering. Her energy captures your attention the moment she opens her mouth. If you're looking for someone with passion and integrity, TK is it." – **Valarie**

"You gave these kids hope. You made them feel like they could accomplish anything. And, now I listen to you and you motivate me. You empower people!" – **Zenia**

"I have not met TK in person, but reading through her writing, her zest, energy and enthusiasm is contagious. I got a boost from her writing." – **Queen**

PLAN THE LIFE YOU WANT

A 7-Step Plan To Achieve Your Goals

TK Owens

www.ingramcontent.com/pod-product-compliance
Lightning Source LLC
Chambersburg PA
CBHW070206100426
42743CB00013B/3068